Getting Started

Carefully remove the three maps from the center of this book to begin.

Political Map

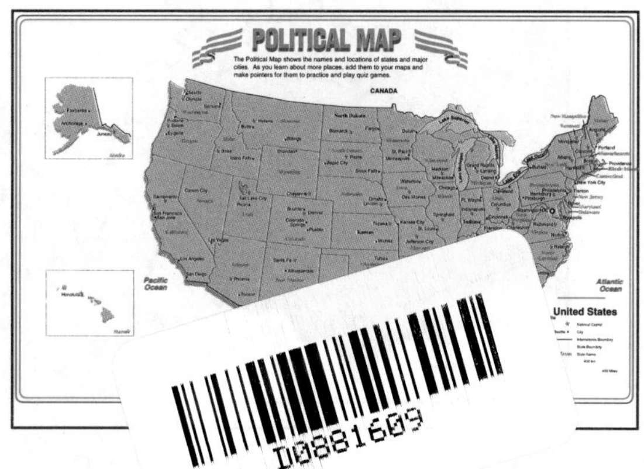

This map shows the locations and the names of:

- states
- capitals
- major cities
- other important sites

Political maps emphasize places with political significance, including boundary lines that separate states and countries.

Physical Map

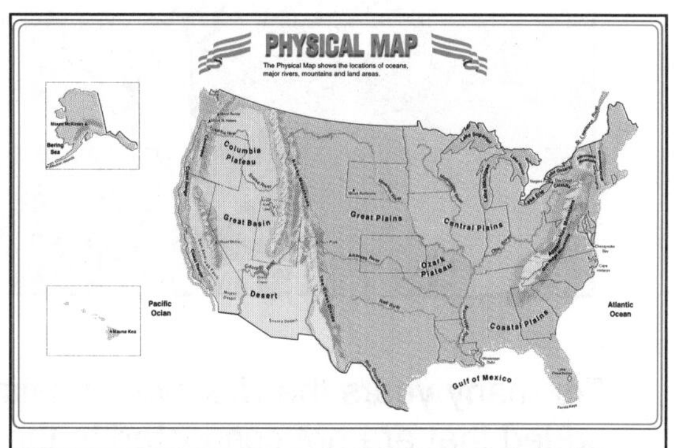

This map shows the locations and the names of:

- oceans, islands
- mountains, plateaus
- lakes, rivers
- bays, gulfs, capes
- deserts, plains
- natural wonders

Physical maps emphasize places that are natural rather than man-made.

Some use colors or shadings to show elevation or land forms.

Practice Map

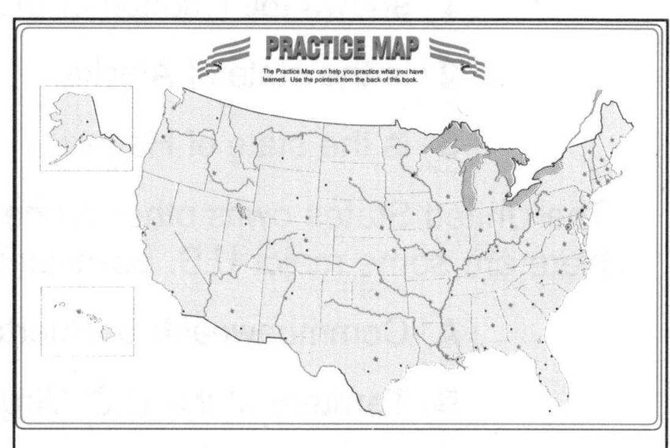

This map will let you practice what you learn.

The practice map can also be used to play geography games with your friends and family. See page 10 for instructions for the games.

As you do the activites on pages 2-9, use the maps as references. Any time a state, city, river, or mountain is mentioned, find it on one of the maps.

Where Is the United States of America?

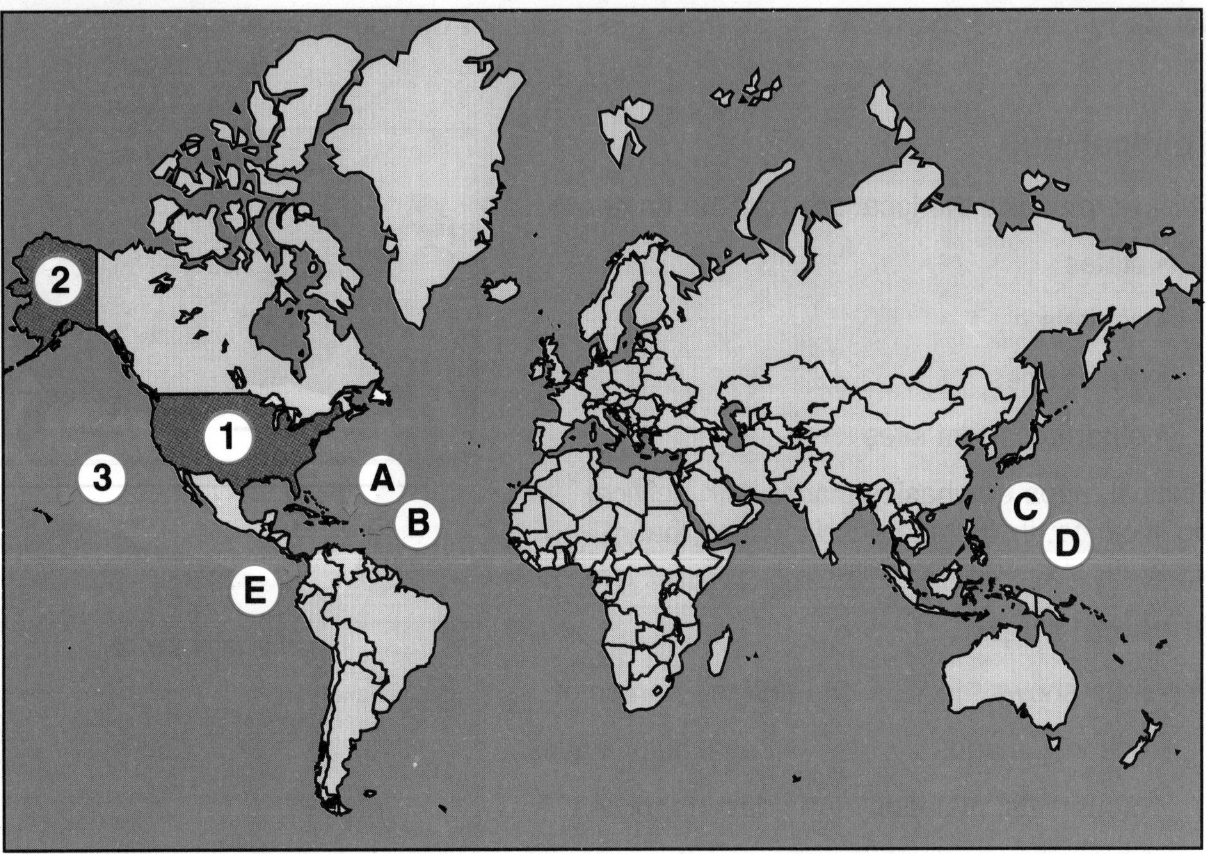

For many years the U.S. was a nation of 48 connected states. In 1959 two states were added that are not connected to the rest. Alaska is separated from the "lower 48" by Canada. Hawaii is separated from the mainland by over 2000 miles of ocean. Now, there are 50 states.

(1) shows the location of the 48 "contiguous" states of the United States.

(2) is the state of Alaska.

(3) is the state of Hawaii.

The United States owns other properties around the world, but they are not states. Here are some major U.S. possessions:

(A) Commonwealth of Puerto Rico

(B) Territory of the U.S. Virgin Islands

(C) Commonwealth of Northern Marianas

(D) Territory of Guam

(E) The Panama Canal (In 1999, the canal will be given to the country of Panama)

4144

How Does the U.S. Measure Up?

The Big Four Countries in Size

There are three countries that are bigger in area than the United States. Can you guess which ones they are? Can you recognize them below, based on an outline of their shapes? Write the names of the countries below each picture. You can check your answers on the inside back cover.

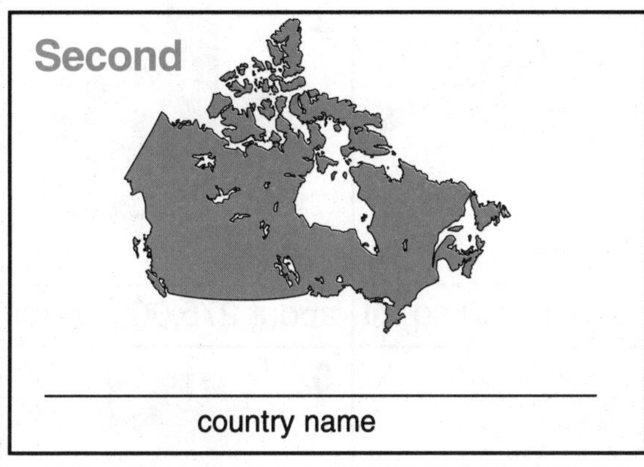

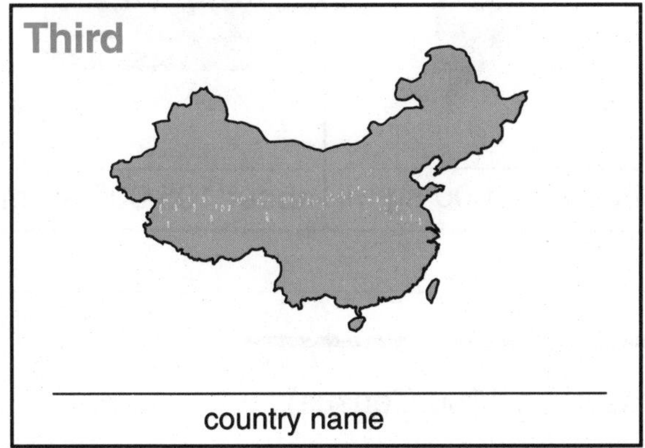

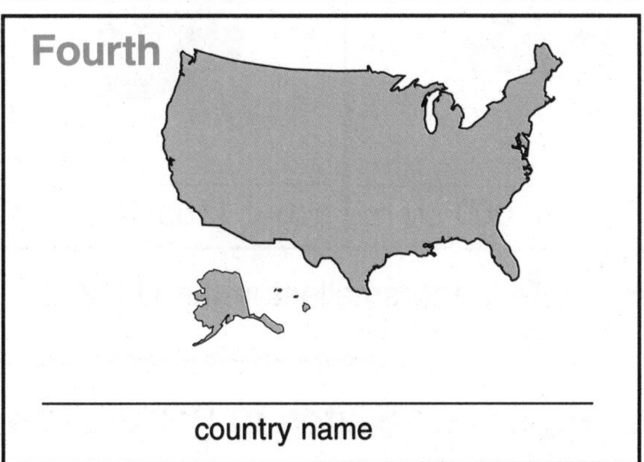

The Big Three Countries in Population

There are two countries with more people than the United States. Can you recognize them?

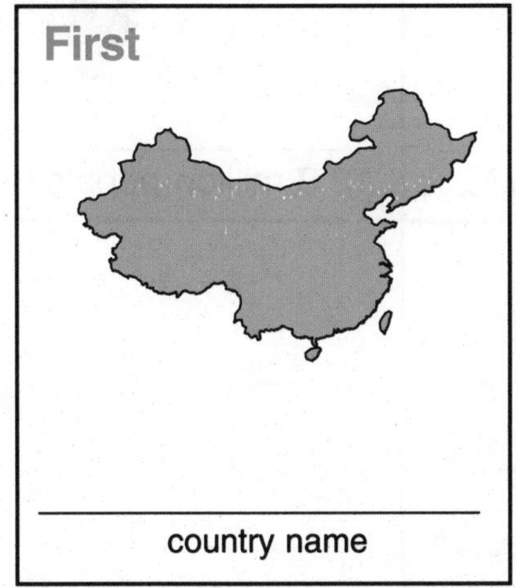

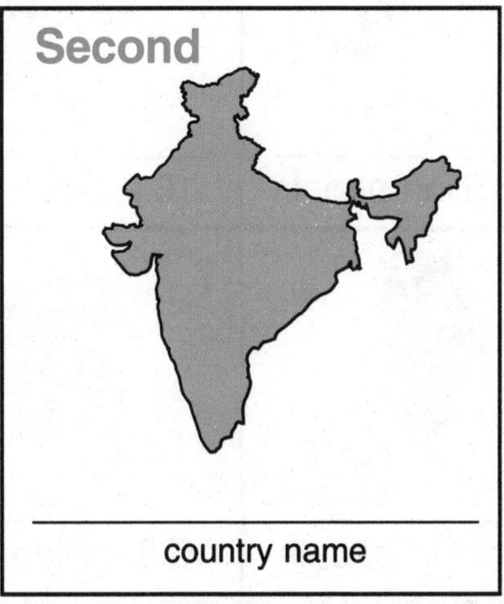

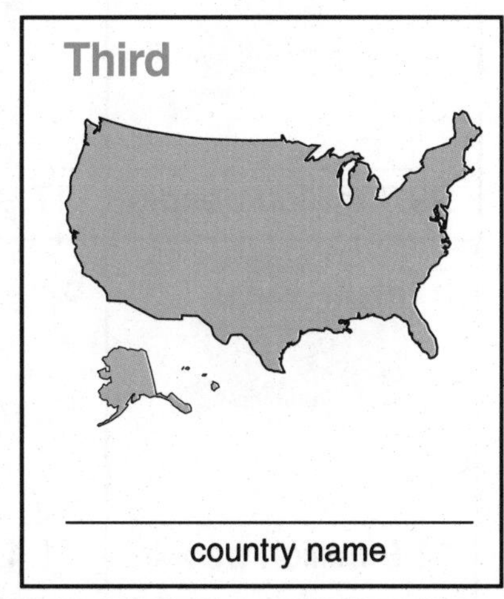

How Do the States Compare?

Look for these states on your map.

The Big Eight States in Area

Can you recognize the 8 states that are over 100,000 square miles?
Write their names on the lines.

1	2	3	4
______ about 575,000 sq mi	______ about 275,000 sq mi	______ about 175,000 sq mi	______ about 150,000 sq mi
5	**6**	**7**	**8**
______ about 120,000 sq mi	______ about 115,000 sq mi	______ about 110,000 sq mi	______ about 105,000 sq mi

Which state is the smallest in the U.S.A.? ____________________

The Big Seven States in Population (Based on 1990 Census)

Can you recognize the 7 states with more than 10 million people?
Write their names on the lines.

1	2	3	4
______ 29.7 million people	______ 17.9 million people	______ 16.9 million people	______ 12.9 million people
5	**6**	**7**	
______ 11.8 million people	______ 11.4 million people	______ 10.8 million people	

U.S. Population

Look for these states on your map.

How Do U.S. Cities Compare?

Here are the eight U.S. cities that have 1 million people or more, listed in alphabetical order.

See if you can rank them in order (1- 8) of population. Use **1** for the city with the most people.

After you have made your best estimates of the ranking, check your answers on the inside back cover.

Cities with the most people:	Rank in terms of population:
Chicago	_____
Dallas	_____
Detroit	_____
Houston	_____
Los Angeles	_____
New York City	_____
Philadelphia	_____
San Diego	_____

Another Way of Looking at Population

A state might have lots of people, but plenty of room for them. A smaller state could have fewer people, and still be crowded. The number of people per square mile is called the "population density." The state with the highest population density didn't even make the Big Seven list on page 4. See if you can guess the answers to these questions:

Which U.S. state has the **highest** population density?

____

This state has about **1000** people per square mile

Which U.S. state has the **lowest** population density?

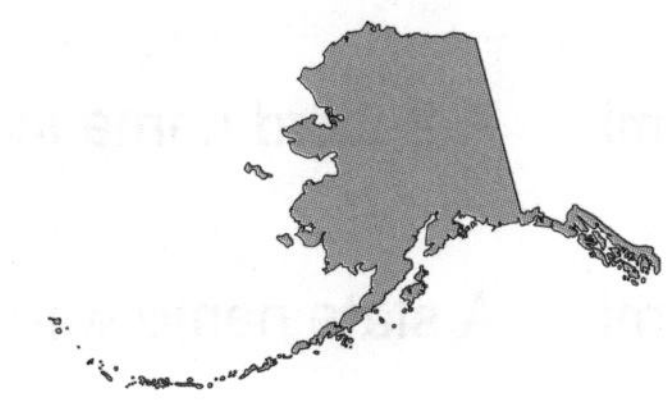

____

This state has about **1** person per square mile

The most crowded area in the U.S. isn't a state or a city. It has almost 10,000 people per square mile. Can you name it?

____

Something About Water?

The Biggest Lakes

Here's a little trick to help you remember the names of the Great Lakes. The first letters of the names spell the word HOMES. Can you name the Great Lakes? One of the big maps in this book will help you with any you can't remember.

H ______________________

O ______________________

M ______________________

E ______________________

S ______________________

The Longest Rivers

See if you can name the U.S. rivers that are longer than 1000 miles from the hints below:

Rank	Length	Hint	
1	2340 mi	The letter S appears 4 times.	M ______________
2	2315 mi	S is in this one only twice.	M ______________
3	1900 mi	A 2-word name in Spanish.	R _______ G ________
4	1450 mi	A state name with a K in it.	A ______________
5	459 mi	Denver is its capital.	C ______________
6	1290 mi	The name of a color.	R ______________
7	1243 mi	Part of the U.S. capital's name.	C ______________
8	1038 mi	A slithering animal.	S ______________

Important Mountains in the U.S.

Where Would You find?

State:

1. The highest mountain in the United States — Mount McKinley - 20,320 feet above sea level. ____________

2. The tallest mountain from its base to its top — Mauna Kea - 33,476 feet tall, but only 13,796 feet are above sea level. ____________

3. The volcano that blew its top in 1980 — Mt. Saint Helens. ____________

4. The highest mountain in the 48 contiguous states — Mt. Whitney - 14,494 feet. ____________

5. The mountain that has been carved to show the faces of four U.S. Presidents — Mt. Rushmore. ____________

6. The mountain you can drive to the top of — Pike's Peak - 14,000+ feet. ____________

Name the Mountain Range

Mountain Range:

1. The range often referred to as the "Continental Divide." ____________

2. The mountain range that the pioneers had to cross to get into California. ____________

3. The mountains that span all the way from New York to Georgia. ____________

Time Zones

You know that the earth turns or rotates. You may not have known that it rotates east to west. This means that people living on the east coast of the U.S. see the sunrise or the sunset before the people who live on the west coast.

To allow clocks to make sense wherever you are in the world, the earth has been divided into 24 time zones. Each time zone is one hour earlier than the time zone to the east.

When you look at the map below, you will notice that the imaginary time zone lines are jagged. This is so population centers on the lines would not be divided into two time zones. Think how confusing it would be if a friend on the other side of town were in a different time zone?

The time zone map shows that there are four time zones in the contiguous 48 states. The time difference between New York and California is three hours. Alaska is one hour earlier than California, and Hawaii is two hours earlier.

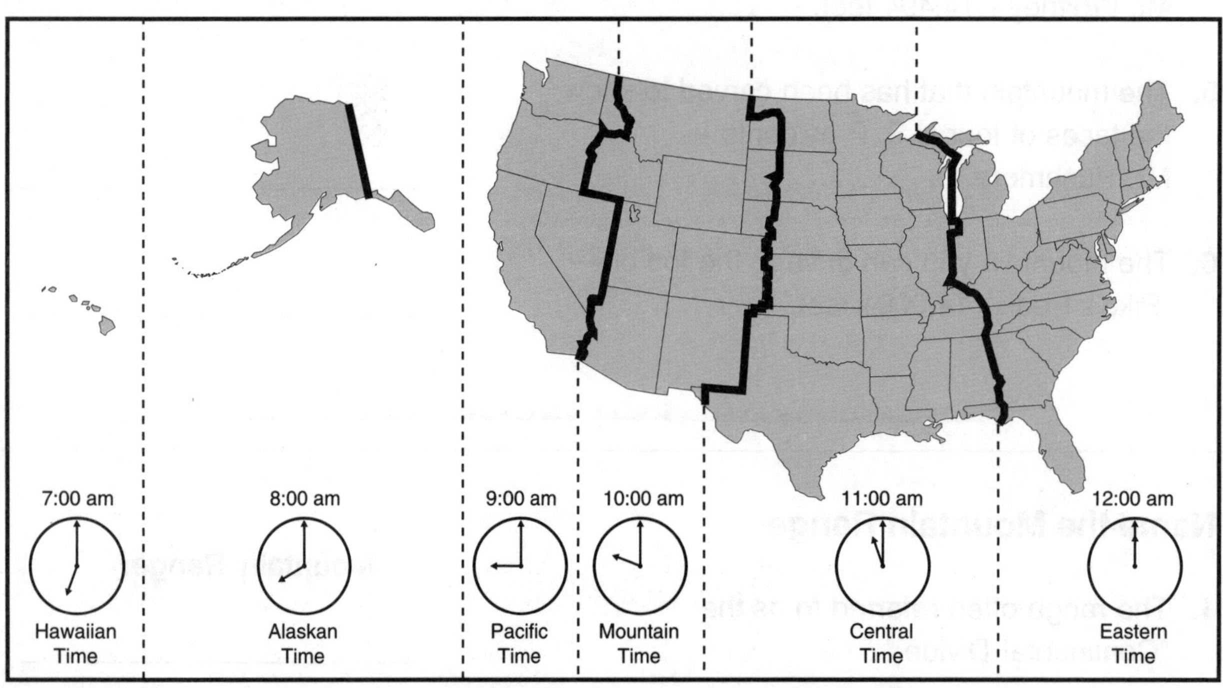

When it is 12:00 noon in California, what time will it be in the following locations? Use your political map to find the locations of places you are not sure about. Then compare the locations to the time zone map above.

California	12:00 noon	Louisiana	________	Hawaii	________
New York	________	Alaska	________	Eastern South Dakota	________
Colorado	________	Maine	________	Western Tennessee	________

Your Personal Geography

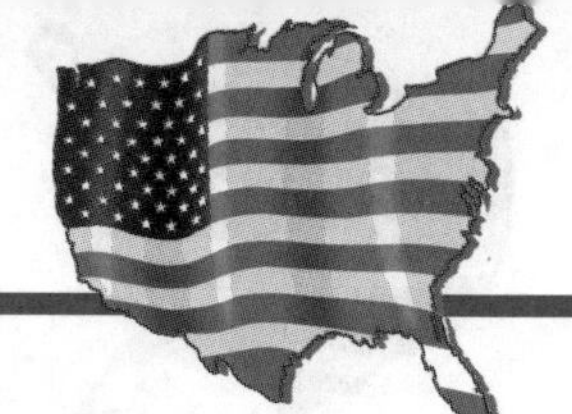

Fill in the blanks below to make a profile of the place where you live. You may have to use some local maps and other references to get all the information.

Your state: ____________________

Population: ____________________

State capital: ____________________

Distance: ____________________

Your city/town: ____________________

Population: ____________________

Your elevation: ____________________

Nearest big city: ____________________

Distance: ____________________

Nearest river: ____________________

Distance: ____________________

Nearest mountain: ____________________

Distance: ____________________

Nearest lake: ____________________

Distance: ____________________

Nearest ocean: ____________________

Distance: ____________________

Draw the basic shape of your state. Show and label the places you describe on the left. For those places that are outside the state, draw an arrow pointing to their location with the distance written by the arrow. You may want to add other important places in your state.

If your state is wider than it is long, you can make your drawing sideways in the box below:

Do you know your

- state motto: ____________________
- state nickname: ____________________
- state bird: ____________________
- state flower: ____________________
- time zone: ____________________

Geography Practice That's Fun

The Pointers on pages 25-31 cover 8 categories of geographical information. Use them with your Practice Map to increase your knowledge of U. S. Geography.

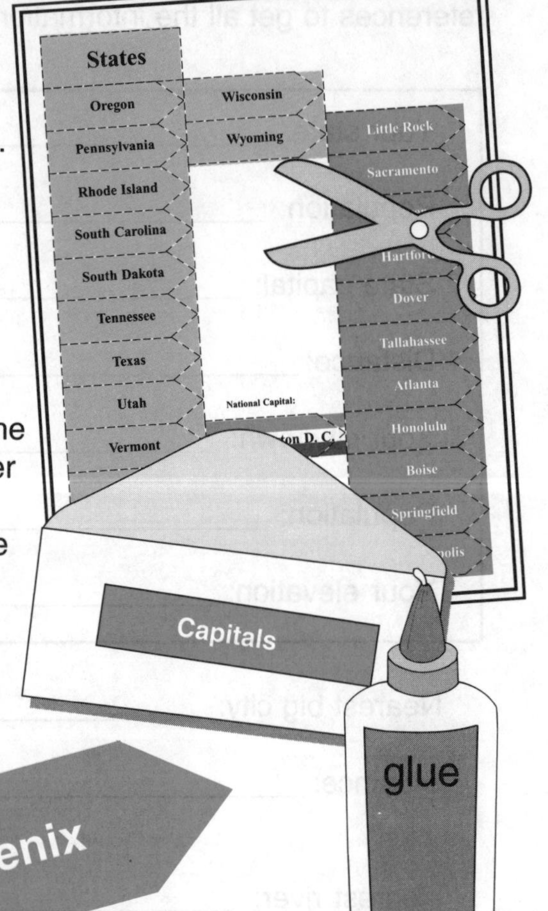

Prepare the Pointers for Use

You will need 8 envelopes, scissors, and glue

1. Cut out the Pointers and the category labels.
2. Glue a label on each of the 8 envelopes.
3. Store each set of Pointers in the envelope labeled in the same color.

Practice for One Can be Fun

- Pick a category of Pointers. Lay the pointers in the correct places on the Practice Map. Use the other two maps and the answer key to check your placements. Say what you are doing out loud like this - "Mount St. Helens is in Washington State." This will help you to remember what you learn.
- Take two categories of Pointers and match them, such as:

  states and capitals

  states and cities

  states and natural features

Games for Two or More

- One player or team picks a category for the other team to place on the Practice Map. Decide if players get to look at the Reference Maps. Set a time limit. Score a point for every Pointer that is correctly placed within the time limit.
- Pick a category. Players or teams take turns drawing and placing a Pointer. Decide on a scoring system, for example:

  5 points for each Pointer placed correctly without looking at a Reference Map.

  2 points for each Pointer placed correctly with the use of a Reference Map.

  If a player cannot answer a question, the next player gets a chance to answer it. For a correct answer, that player gets the points and another turn.

- Create your own game rules - anything goes!

As you learn the names and locations of more places, add them to your maps and make pointers for them. Continue adding to what you know about U.S. Geography.

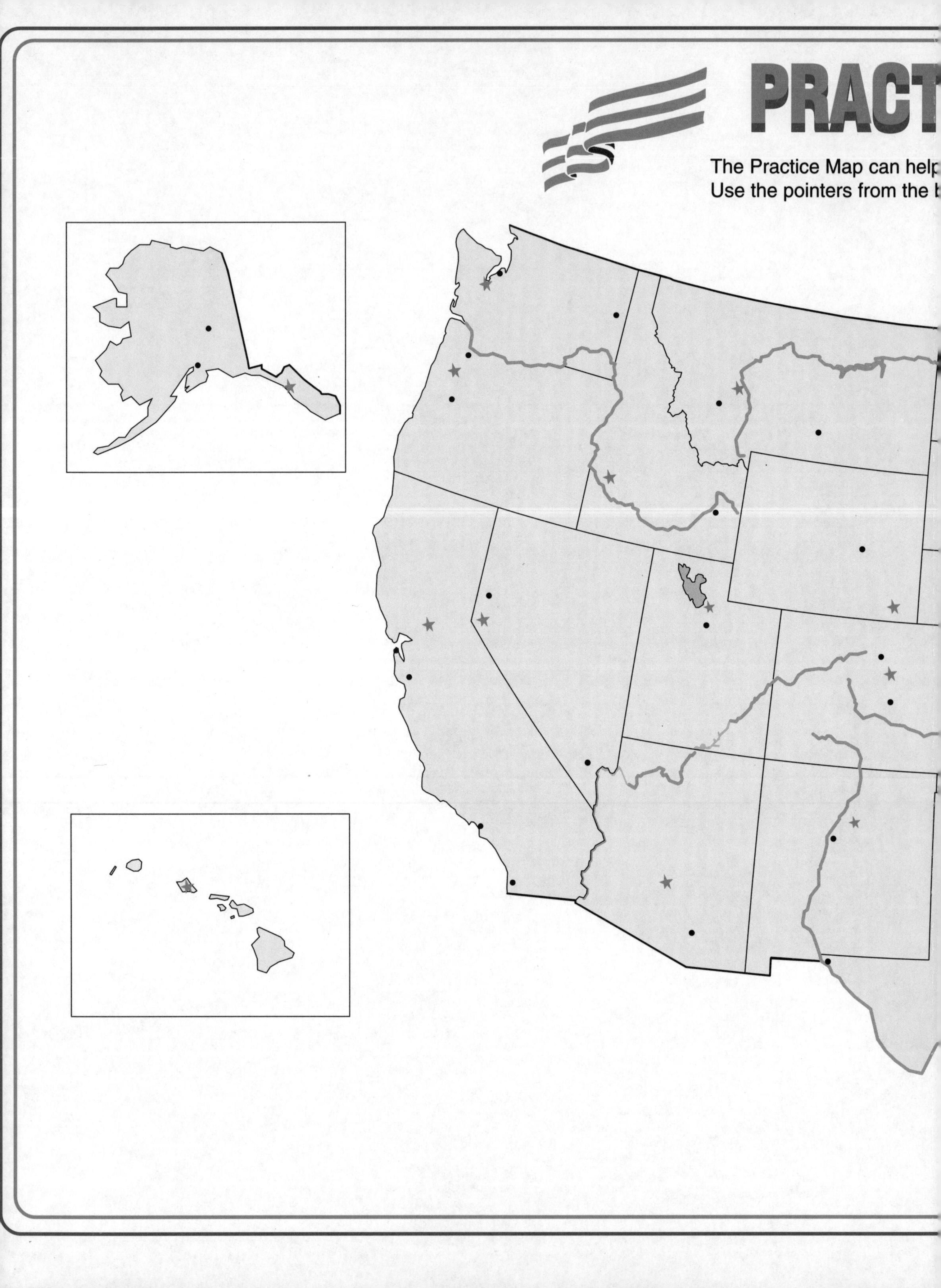
PRACT
The Practice Map can help
Use the pointers from the b

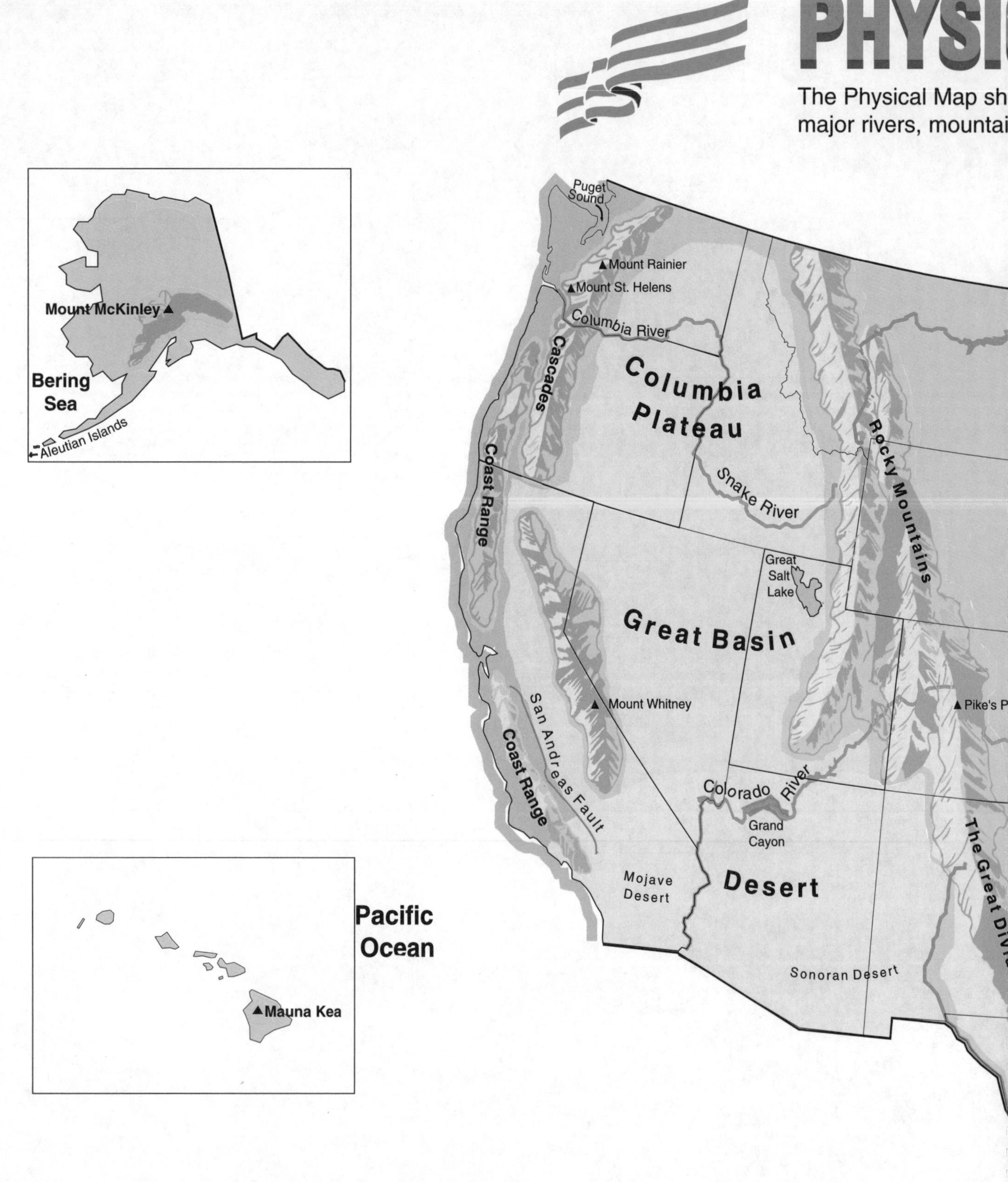

The Physical Map
major rivers,
Puget Sound
Mount Rainier
Mount St. Helens
Columbia River
Cascades
Columbia Plateau
Coast Range
Snake River
Rocky Mountains
Great Salt Lake
Great Basin
Mount Whitney
San Andreas Fault
Coast Range
Colorado River
Grand Cayon
Mojave Desert
Desert
Sonoran Desert
The Great
Mount McKinley
Bering Sea
Aleutian Islands
Pacific Ocean
Mauna Kea

POLITI

The Political Map shows the nam

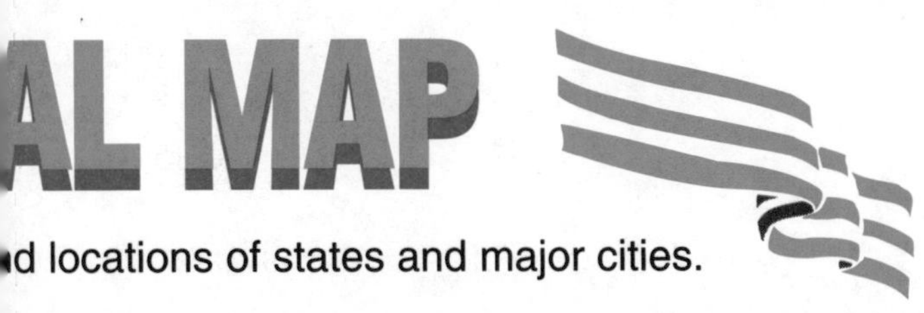

AL MAP
d locations of states and major cities.

CANADA

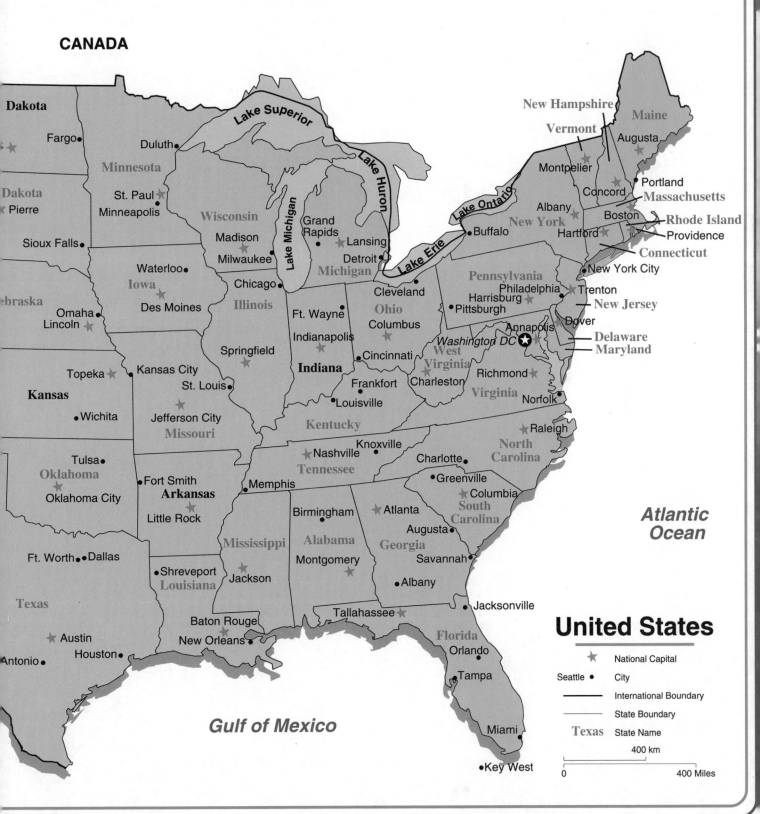

Dakota
Fargo
Duluth
Lake Superior
Lake Huron
Lake Michigan
Lake Ontario
Lake Erie
Minnesota
St. Paul
Minneapolis
Dakota
Pierre
Sioux Falls
Wisconsin
Madison
Milwaukee
Grand Rapids
Lansing
Detroit
Michigan
Waterloo
Iowa
Des Moines
Chicago
Illinois
Omaha
Lincoln
braska
Ft. Wayne
Indiana
Indianapolis
Springfield
Cleveland
Ohio
Columbus
Cincinnati
Topeka
Kansas City
St. Louis
Kansas
Wichita
Jefferson City
Missouri
Frankfort
Louisville
Kentucky
Tulsa
Oklahoma
Oklahoma City
Fort Smith
Arkansas
Little Rock
Memphis
Nashville
Knoxville
Tennessee
Ft. Worth
Dallas
Shreveport
Louisiana
Texas
Austin
Houston
Antonio
Mississippi
Jackson
Baton Rouge
New Orleans
Birmingham
Alabama
Montgomery
Atlanta
Georgia
Augusta
Savannah
Albany
Tallahassee
Jacksonville
Florida
Orlando
Tampa
Miami
Key West
Gulf of Mexico
Charlotte
North Carolina
Raleigh
Greenville
Columbia
South Carolina
West Virginia
Charleston
Richmond
Virginia
Norfolk
Washington DC
Annapolis
Dover
Delaware
Maryland
Pennsylvania
Harrisburg
Pittsburgh
Philadelphia
Trenton
New Jersey
New York City
Buffalo
New York
Albany
Hartford
Connecticut
Providence
Rhode Island
Boston
Massachusetts
Concord
Portland
Montpelier
Vermont
New Hampshire
Maine
Augusta
Atlantic Ocean

United States

National Capital
Seattle • City
International Boundary
State Boundary
Texas State Name
400 km
0 400 Miles

AL MAP
ne locations of oceans,
d land areas.
St. Lawrence River
Lake Superior
Lake Huron
Lake Michigan
Adirondack Mountains
White Mountains
Hudson River
Lake Ontario
Niagara Falls
Erie Canal
Catskills
Lake Erie
Missouri River
Mount Rushmore
Mississippi River
Great Plains
Central Plains
Appalachian Mountains
Blue Ridge Mountains
Ohio River
Chesapeake Bay
Arkansas River
Ozark Plateau
Cape Hatteras
Red River
Mississippi River
Atlantic Ocean
Coastal Plains
Mississippi Delta
Rio Grande River
Lake Okeechobee
Florida Keys

CE MAP

practice what you have learned.
of this book.

States

Alabama	Illinois	Missouri
Alaska	Indiana	Montana
Arizona	Iowa	Nebraska
Arkansas	Kansas	Nevada
California	Kentucky	New Hampshire
Colorado	Louisiana	New Jersey
Connecticut	Maine	New Mexico
Delaware	Maryland	New York
Florida	Massachusetts	North Carolina
Georgia	Michigan	North Dakota
Hawaii	Minnesota	Ohio
Idaho	Mississippi	Oklahoma

States	Capitals	
Oregon	Wisconsin	Phoenix
Pennsylvania	Wyoming	Little Rock
Rhode Island		Sacramento
South Carolina		Denver
South Dakota		Hartford
Tennessee		Dover
Texas		Tallahassee
Utah	National Capital:	Atlanta
Vermont	Washington D.C.	Honolulu
Virginia	State Capitals:	Boise
Washington	Montgomery	Springfield
West Virginia	Juneau	Indianapolis

4144

Capitals

Des Moines	Lincoln	Providence
Frankfort	Carson City	Columbia
Topeka	Concord	Pierre
Baton Rouge	Trenton	Nashville
Augusta	Santa Fe	Austin
Annapolis	Albany	Salt Lake City
Boston	Raleigh	Montpelier
Lansing	Bismarck	Richmond
Saint Paul	Columbus	Olympia
Jackson	Oklahoma City	Charleston
Jefferson City	Salem	Madison
Helena	Harrisburg	Cheyenne

Biggest Cities	States Most Famous For	Natural Features
New York City	Potatoes	Cape Cod
Los Angeles	Peaches	Florida Keys
Chicago	Auto Industry	Chesapeake Bay
Houston	Pineapples	Mojave Desert
Philadephia	Steel	Niagara Falls
San Diego	"The Big Apple"	Grand Canyon
Detroit	Yellowstone Park	San Andreas Fault
Dallas	Movie Industry	Aleutian Islands
Phoenix	Kodiak Bears	Mount St. Helens
San Antonio	Racehorses	Ozark Plateau
San Jose	15,000+ Lakes	Cape Hatteras
Indianapolis	Disney World	Mississippi Delta

Bodies of Water	Important Rivers	Mountains and Ranges
Pacific Ocean	Mississippi River	Mt. McKinley
Atlantic Ocean	Missouri River	Mt. Whitney
Gulf of Mexico	Rio Grande	Mt. Rainier
Lake Superior	Colorado River	Pike's Peak
Bering Sea	Arkansas River	Rockies
Lake Michigan	Red River	Sierra Nevada
Lake Huron	Columbia River	Coast Range
Lake Erie	Ohio River	Adirondacks
Lake Ontario	Snake River	Catskills
Great Salt Lake	St. Lawrence River	Mt. St. Helens
Lake Okeechobee	Hudson River	Appalachians
Puget Sound	Erie Canal	Cascades